God
can handle it
...for Fathers

God
can handle it
...for Fathers

Compiled and Edited by
Jim Gallery

BRIGHTON BOOKS
Nashville, TN 37211

ISBN 1-887655-95-6

The ideas expressed in this book (but not scripture verses) are not, in all cases, exact quotations, as some have been edited for clarity and brevity. In all cases, the author has attempted to maintain the speaker's original intent. In some cases, material for this book was obtained from secondary sources, primarily print media. While every effort was made to ensure the accuracy of these sources, the accuracy cannot be guaranteed. For additions, deletions, corrections or clarifications in future editions of this text, please write BRIGHTON BOOKS.

Typesetting by Sue Gerdes

Cover Design by Tal Howell

Printed in the United States of America
1 2 3 4 5 6 7 8 9 10 • 99 00 01 02 03 04

To My Father
who did what was required of him —
to act justly; love mercy; and walk humbly
with his God

Table of Contents

A Message to Readers

A man may fill many roles in life, but no role is greater than that of father. Bill Cosby once observed, "Nothing I've ever done has given me more joys and rewards than being a father to my children." Dads everywhere know the feeling.

Along with the joys of fatherhood come the sobering responsibilities of being a good parent. Every father knows the awesomeness of the task...and so does God in heaven. The apostle Paul reminds us that "God will take care of everything you need" (Philippians 4:19, THE MESSAGE). Thus, God stands ready, willing and able to help good men become great fathers.

If you're lucky enough to be a father, (or if you're about to become one), pay careful attention to the ideas in this book. Read God's Word and claim His promises. Learn from the voices of experience that appear on these pages. Vow that with God's help, you will become the very best dad you can be. And be comforted by the fact that nothing is going to happen today that you and *your* Father can't handle.

1

The Gift of God — Children

The Psalmist declares, "Behold, children are a gift of the Lord..."(127:3a NIV). Jesus tells us that God is in the business of giving us good gifts (Luke 11:13) and what greater gift can He give than children?

Kate Douglas Wiggin correctly observes, "Every child born into the world is a new thought of God, an ever-fresh and radiant possibility." But sometimes the hustle and bustle of life obscures this wonderful truth.

Dad, always remember that your child is a gift of God, brimming with potential. So take a few moments to give thanks to the Giver, and above all, take very good care of the gift.

A baby is God's opinion
that the world should
go on.

Carl Sandburg

...stop and consider God's wonders.
Job 37:14

Children are the hands by which we take
hold of heaven.

Henry Ward Beecher

Children are God's small interpreters.

John Greenleaf Whittier

Every child comes with the message
that God is not yet discouraged of man.

Tagore

*"For unto us a child is born,
to us a Son is given...."
Isaiah 9:6*

A child, more than all other gifts that earth can offer to declining man, brings hope with it and forward-looking thoughts.

William Wordsworth

Jesus said, "Let the little children come to me, and do not hinder them, for the kingdom of heaven belongs to such as these."
Matthew 19:14

Kids are great. They are exciting.
Their potential is simply phenomenal. And in
any given family there is the potential
to change the world for God.

Maxine Hancock

Every child who comes into the world
presents a new possibility for lifting
the destiny of the human race.

Anna B. Mow

Life is a flame that is always burning itself
out, but it catches fire again every time
a child is born.

George Bernard Shaw

*"Whoever welcomes one of these little children
in my name [Jesus] welcomes me...."*
Mark 9:36-37

God supervised your child's construction even down to the tips of his fingers.

Cliff Schimmels

I praise you because I am fearfully and wonderfully made...
Psalm 139:14

W e can't form our children on our own
concepts, we must take them as God
gives them to us.

Goethe

C hildren are today's investments and
tomorrow's dividend.

Unknown

E veryone's life is a fairy tale written
by God's fingers.

Hans Christian Andersen

*...bring them up in the training and instruction
of the Lord.
Ephesians 6:4*

How badly America needs husbands and fathers who are committed to their families — men who are determined to succeed in this important responsibility.

James Dobson

...your hearts must be fully committed to the Lord our God....
I Kings 8:61

There is no more vital calling or vocation
for men than fathering.

John R. Throop

A father is a man who is always learning
how to love. He knows that his love
must grow and change because
his children change.

Tim Hansel

What is a father? To his child, he is
strength, security, example, and number-one
friend. It's a great calling, so celebrate the gift
of your fatherhood.

Unknown

A child's glory is his father.
Proverbs 17:6b TLB

What was wonderful about childhood
was that everything in it was a wonder.
It was not merely a world full of miracles,
it was a miraculous world.

G. K. Chesterton

By profession I am a soldier and take pride
in that fact, but I am prouder to be a father.

General Douglas MacArthur

Directly after God in Heaven comes Papa.

Wolfgang Amadeus Mozart

Children are our most valuable resource.

Herbert Hoover

Behold, children are a gift of the Lord....
Psalm 127:3 NASB

2

Prayer is Power

Raising children to become successful adults requires every resource Dads can muster. There is no more powerful tool than prayer. "The most effective thing we can do for our children and families is pray for them," counsels speaker and author Anthony Evans.

The gospel writer Mark records, "The next morning Jesus awoke long before daybreak and went out alone into the wilderness to pray" (1:35). If Jesus placed a priority on prayer, Dads should follow His example.

Take a knee, Dads. It's time to put some power into your parenting.

Prayer accomplishes more than anything else.

Bill Bright

This is the confidence we have in approaching God: that if we ask anything according to his will, he hears us.
1 John 5:14

Pray every day for your children.
This is an area where Christian parents
don't have an option.

Dick Hagstrom

To talk to his children about God, a man
needs to first talk to God about his children.

Edwin Louis Cole

The family that prays together stays together.

Anonymous

...with all prayer and petition,
pray at all times in the Spirit....
Ephesians 6:18 NASB

Devote yourselves to prayer, keeping alert in it with an attitude of thanksgiving.

The Apostle Paul

Do not be anxious about anything, but in every-thing, by prayer and petition, with thanksgiving, present your requests to God.
Philippians 4:6

For the eyes of the Lord are on the righteous
and his ears are attentive to their prayers.

The Apostle Peter

The best parenting skills come most naturally
when the parents are on their knees.

Julie Bakke

Happy is the child who happens in upon
his parent from time to time to see him
on his knees...or going aside regularly,
to keep times with the Lord.

Larry Christenson

*...he offered up prayers...and he was
heard because of his reverent submission.
Hebrews 5:7*

Do not pray for easy lives.
Pray to be stronger men!
Do not pray for tasks
equal to your powers. Pray
for powers equal
to your tasks.

Keith L. Brooks

When I called, you answered me; you made me
bold and stouthearted.
Psalm 138:3

Secret prayer is the secret of prayer.

Armin Gesswein

But when you pray, go into your room,
close the door and pray to your Father,
who is unseen. Then your Father, who sees
what is done in secret, will reward you.

Jesus

O Lord...build me a son whose heart will
be clear, whose goal will be high, a son who
will master himself before he seeks to master
other men; one who will reach into the future,
yet never forget the past.

General Douglas MacArthur

*You will seek Me and find Me when you
seek for Me with all your heart.
Jeremiah 29:13 NASB*

Show me the path where I should walk, O Lord; point out the right road for me to follow.

The Psalmist

I will answer them before they even call to me. While they are still talking to me about their needs, I will go ahead and answer their prayers!
Isaiah 65:24 TLB

3

Spiritual Growth for Spiritual Leadership

Helping a child mature spiritually is an awesome responsibility. Fathers are called upon to provide spiritual leadership; to do so, they must lead by example.

Fathers who seek to guide their families along the path of spiritual growth must, of necessity, walk that path themselves. As Glen Wheeler correctly notes, "A child is not likely to find a father in God unless he finds something of God in his father."

Dad, your child, like every child, is on a spiritual journey; but he needs your help. To provide spiritual leadership, you, too, must make the journey. Whatever you do, don't miss this opportunity to lead...and to grow.

You cannot honor your
family without nurturing
your own sense of
personal value and honor.

Stephen Covey

...Let us press on to know the Lord....
Hosea 6:3 NASB

Creating a warm, caring, supportive, encouraging environment is probably the most important thing you can do for your family.

Stephen Covey

A happy family is but an earlier heaven.

Sir John Browing

Money can build or buy a house. Add love to that and you have a home. Add God to that and you have a temple. You have "a little colony of the kingdom of heaven."

Anne Ortland

Unless the Lord builds the house,
its builders labor in vain.
Psalm 127:1

I realized that if my children were to know Christ's love, then I, as their father, needed to experience more of Christ's love and make that love visible.

John Drescher

Happy are those whose hearts are pure,
for they shall see God.
Matthew 5:8 TLB

A child identifies his parents with God,
whether adults want the role or not.
Most children "see" God the way
they perceive their earthly fathers.

James Dobson

Children miss nothing in sizing up their
parents. If you are only half-convinced
of your beliefs, they will quickly discern
that fact.

James Dobson

Any child will learn to worship God
who lives his daily life with adults
who worship Him.

Anna B. Mow

*Therefore be imitators of God
as beloved children.
Ephesians 5:1 NASB*

It is actually impossible to forsake our own spiritual development in favor of someone else's.

M. Scott Peck

…as the Spirit of the Lord works within us, we become more and more like him….
2 Corinthians 3:18

It is right to be contented with what we have, never with what we are.

James Mackintosh

The greatness of work is inside man.

Pope John Paul II

Aim at heaven and you will get earth thrown in. Aim at earth and you get neither.

C. S. Lewis

For he satisfies the thirsty and fills the hungry with good things.
Psalm 107:9

Lord, help me to remember that nothing is going to happen to me today that you and I together can't handle.

Anonymous

I will lift up mine eyes unto the hills, from whence cometh my help. My help cometh from the Lord, which made heaven and earth.
Psalm 121:1-2

My children make me totally dependent upon God. I can do my best, but the ultimate results are out of my control. My children help me run to God, the only safe place to be.

David Grant

It is for us to make the effort.
The result is in God's hands.

Anonymous

Being a father is teaching me that when I am criticized, injured or afraid, there is a Father who is ready to comfort me.

Max Lucado

...let the heart of them rejoice that seek the Lord, seek the Lord, and his strength: seek his face evermore.
Psalm 105:3-4

If you seek the Lord your God, you will find him if you look for him with all your heart and with all your soul.

Moses

The Lord is good to those who wait for Him,
to the person who seeks Him.
Lamentations 3:25 NASB

All scripture is inspired of God and is useful to teach us what is true.

The Apostle Paul

It is less important to ask a Christian what he or she believes about the Bible than to inquire what he or she does with it.

Lesslie Newbigin

To be a successful parent, we must first love the Word of God.

George Sweeting

I will instruct thee and teach thee in the way which thou shalt go; I will guide thee with mine eye.
Psalm 32:8 KJV

Trust in yourself and you are doomed to disappointment; trust in money and you may have it taken from you, but trust in God, and you are never to be confounded in time or eternity.

D. L. Moody

It is better to take refuge in the Lord
than to trust in man.
Psalm 118:8

The father is the head of a unit of people launched on an exploration of life and all the things God has placed in the world for us to discover and enjoy.

Gordon MacDonald

It's never too late for a father to start being a leader in his home. But it's never too soon, either.

Barry St. Clair

He that thinketh he leadeth, but hath no one following him — he is only out for a walk.

Unknown

You will make known to me the path of life....
Psalm 16:11 NASB

My primary role is not to be the boss and just look good, but to be a servant leader who enables and enhances my family to be their best.

Tim Hansel

*...whoever wants to be great among you
must be your servant....
Matthew 20:26*

4

The Hunger to be Understood

Adults want to be understood and so do children. Stephen Covey speaks to all ages when he says, "The deepest hunger of the human heart is to be understood."

These words echo the sentiment of the writer of Proverbs: "How much better to get wisdom than gold, to choose understanding rather than silver" (16:16).

Dads, remember that you fulfill a deep human need by listening with an understanding heart to your children. When you do, your rewards will be greater than gold.

Opportunities for meaningful communication between fathers and sons must be created. And it's work to achieve.

James Doubloon

Whatever you do, work at it with all your heart,
as working for the Lord, not for men.
Colossians 3:23

The first duty of love is to listen.

Paul Tillich

Don't offer solutions to complaints,
just listen.

Gary Smalley

Part of good communication is listening
with the eyes well as with the ears.

Josh McDowell

*I love God because he listened to me....
Psalm 116:1 THE MESSAGE*

Be a good listener. Your ears will never get you in trouble.

Frank Tyger

He that hath ears to hear, let him hear.
Matthew 11:15 KJV

Communication begins with
understanding others.

Anonymous

The man of true greatness never loses
his child's heart.

Mencius

It is a wise father who knows his own child.
William Shakespeare

The one who knows much says little;
an understanding person remains calm.
Proverbs 17:27 THE MESSAGE

Knowledge speaks, but wisdom listens.

Oliver Wendall Holmes

Be still and know that I am God.
Psalm 46:10

When you listen to your children, you
are paying them a compliment. By listening,
you increase their feelings of self-respect
and self-worth.

Dean & Grace Merrill

The more a child becomes aware of a
father's willingness to listen, the more
a father will begin to hear.

Gordon MacDonald

The quality of a child's relationship with his
or her father seems to be the most important
influence in deciding how that person
will react to the world.

John Nicholson

There is a time to be silent and a time to speak.
Ecclesiastes 3:7

God gave us two ears and one mouth, so we ought to listen twice as much as we speak.

Irish Proverb

*...Everyone should be quick to listen,
slow to speak....*
James 1:19

5

Laughter

Do you remember the delight of chasing the neighborhood ice cream truck for a delicious treat? If you were quick enough, you caught the 'Good Humor' man, and he could brighten up the hottest of summer days.

The 'Good Humor Dad' can brighten up the lives of his children and family because, as we are reminded in Proverbs, "A merry heart doeth good like a medicine" (17:22 KJV). Eugene Peterson translates that verse: "A cheerful disposition is good for your health; gloom and doom leave you bone-tired" (THE MESSAGE).

Victor Borge suggests, "Laughter is the shortest distance between two people." So Dads, get closer to your kids with lots of giggles, a few snickers and an occasional belly-laugh. Your kids will love you for it.

Always laugh when you can; it is cheap medicine. Merriment is a philosophy not well understood. It is the sunny side of existence.

George Gordon Byron

A merry heart doeth good like a medicine....
Proverbs 17:22 KJV

Laughter has no foreign accent.

Paul Lowney

Laughter is the music of the world.

Anonymous

To me, a healthy belly laugh is one
of the most beautiful sounds in the world.

Bennett Cerf

A twinkle in the eye means joy in the heart....
Proverbs 15:30 THE MESSAGE

Humor is a prelude to faith, and laughter is the beginning of prayer.

Reinhold Niebuhr

A merry heart doeth good like a medicine....
Proverbs 17:22 KJV

Laughter is like premium gasoline:
It helps take the knock out of living.

Unknown

When I was a boy of fourteen, my father was so ignorant I could hardly stand to have the old man around. But when I got to be twenty-one, I was astonished at how much he had learned in seven years.

Mark Twain

Humor makes all things tolerable.

Henry Ward Beecher

A twinkle in the eye means joy in the heart....
Proverbs 15:30 THE MESSAGE

Insanity is hereditary.
> You get it from your kids.

Unknown

Every parent believes in heredity
> until the children start acting goofy.

Anonymous

Before I got married, I had six theories
> about bringing up children; now I have
> six children and no theories.

Lord Rochester

A merry heart doeth good like a medicine....
Proverbs 17:22 KJV

Most people are about as happy as they make up their minds to be.

Abraham Lincoln

A twinkle in the eye means joy in the heart....
Proverbs 15:30 THE MESSAGE

Fatherhood is pretending that the gift
you love most is soap-on-a-rope.

Bill Cosby

There are three ways to get something done:
Do it yourself, hire someone,
or forbid your kids to do it.

Monta Crane

Father: A man who can't get on the phone,
into the bathroom, or out of the house.

Anonymous

A merry heart doeth good like a medicine....
Proverbs 17:22 KJV

Many a father wishes he were strong enough to tear a telephone book in two — especially if he has a teenage daughter.

Guy Lombardo

A twinkle in the eye means joy in the heart....
Proverbs 15:30 THE MESSAGE

Fathers are those who give daughters away
to other men who aren't nearly good enough
so they can have grandchildren who
are smarter than anybody's.

Paul Harvey

Most daughters marry men just like their
fathers. Maybe that's why so many mothers
cry at their weddings.

Bruce Wilkinson

A merry heart doeth good like a medicine….
Proverbs 17:22 KJV

Above all, life should be fun.

Anonymous

A twinkle in the eye means joy in the heart....
Proverbs 15:30 THE MESSAGE

A father is someone who carries pictures
where his money used to be.

Unknown

People who say they sleep like a baby
usually don't have one.

Leo Burke

The best time for parents to put the children
to bed is while they still have the strength.

Herman Phillips

A merry heart doeth good like a medicine....
Proverbs 17:22 KJV

Most things have an escape clause, but children are forever.

Lewis Grizzard

A twinkle in the eye means joy in the heart....
Proverbs 15:30 THE MESSAGE

For reasons I can't explain, I really like being a parent. It's just that there's a lot more to it than I expected.

Dave Barry

Children are a great comfort in your old age, and they help you to reach it faster, too.

Lionel Kaufman

Parents: persons who spend half their time worrying how a child will turn out, and the rest of the time wondering when a child will turn in.

Ted Cook

A merry heart doeth good like a medicine....
Proverbs 17:22 KJV

6

Love is a Verb

"...But while he was still a long way off, his father saw him and was filled with compassion for him; he ran to his son, threw his arms around him and kissed him" (Luke 15:20). The prodigal son had done everything wrong yet the unconditional love of his father restored him to a life he was meant to live.

How is love defined? M. Scott Peck writes, "Love is too large, too deep ever to be truly understood or measured or limited with the framework of words." In the final analysis, the *definition* of love is not important, but the *act* of loving is all-important.

A father's responsibility is simple: to love his wife, his children, his family and his friends. The following pages remind dads and non-dads alike that love, however it is defined, is a verb.

No man can possibly know what life means, what the world means, what anything means, until he has a child and loves it.

Lafcadio Hearn

And this I pray, that your love may abound yet more and more....
Philippians 1:9

A father is a man who is always learning
how to love. He knows that his love
must grow and change because
his children change.

Tim Hansel

Children desperately need to know —
and to hear in ways they understand and
remember — that they're loved and valued
by Mom and Dad.

Gary Smalley and Paul Trent

Parenthood is just the world's
most intensive course in love.

Polly Berrien Berends

*Be imitators of God, as beloved children; and
walk in love, just as Christ also loved you....
Ephesians 5:1-2 NASB*

Love is caught, not taught.

Frank Laubach

...let us stop saying we love people; let us really love them, and show it by our actions.
1 John 3:18 TLB

Love doesn't sit there like a stone, it has
to be made like bread; remade all the time;
made new.

Ursula K. LeGuin

Love is active and sincere; courageous;
patient; faithful; prudent; and manly.

Thomas á Kempis

If one wishes to know love, one must live love.

Leo Buscaglia

*Let love and faithfulness never leave you;
bind them around your neck, write them
on the tablet of your heart.
Proverbs 3:3-4*

If love is to produce the emotional, physical and spiritual intimacy it is designed to produce, it must be committed, faithful love.

Josh McDowell

May your fountain be blessed, and may you rejoice in the wife of your youth...may you ever be captivated by her love.
Proverbs 5:18-19

For dad, the most important job is to show everyone in the family that mom comes first.

Harold Myra

The kids should never become
more important than the spouse!

Ted Engstrom

A palace without affection is a poor hovel,
and the leanest hut with love in it is
a palace for the soul.

Robert G. Ingersoll

For the love of Christ controls us....
II Corinthians 5:14 NASB

You will find, as you look back upon your life, that the moments when you have really lived are the moments when you have done things in the spirit of love.

Henry Drummond

And [Jesus] took the children in his arms....
Mark 10:16

The great man is he who does not lose
his child's heart.

Mencius

The ability to love is the heart of the matter.
That is how we must measure our success
or failure at being parents.

Gloria Vanderbilt

When God measures a man, He puts
the tape around the heart instead of the head.

Unknown

He that loveth not knoweth not God;
for God is love.
I John 4:8 KJV

The affirmation of one's own life, happiness, growth, freedom, is rooted in one's capacity to love.

Erich Fromm

Be humble and gentle. Be patient with each other, making allowance for each others's faults because of your love.
Ephesians 4:2 TLB

Children need love, especially when they
do not deserve it.

Harold S. Hulbert

Unconditional love is loving a child
no matter what we expect him to be,
and most difficult, no matter how he acts.

Ross Campbell

If love is freely given and freely accepted
with no strings attached, individual freedom
and responsibility can develop.

Kay Kuzma

*For as high as the heavens are above the earth,
so great is his love for those who fear him.
Psalm 103:11*

Who, being loved, is poor?

Oscar Wilde

Life minus love equals zero.

George Sweeting

It is not a slight thing when they,
who are so fresh from God, love us.

Charles Dickens

Dad, when you come home at night
with only shattered pieces of your dreams,
your little one can mend them like new with
two magic words: "Hi, Dad!"

Alan Beck

Follow the way of love....
I Corinthians 14:1

To be loved, love.

Decimus Maximus Ausonius

*Whoever has my commands and obeys them,
he is the one who loves me. He who loves me
will be loved by my Father, and I too will love
him and show myself to him.*
John 14:21

We do not have to love. We choose to love.

M. Scott Peck

Love is not primarily an emotion,
but an act of will.

Frederick Buechner

Love is an act of will, namely,
both intention and an action.

M. Scott Peck

We love, because He first loved us.

The Apostle John

*As high as heaven is over the earth,
so strong is his love to those who fear him.
Psalm 103:11 THE MESSAGE*

7

Hip, Hip, Hooray!

No one can receive too many pats on the back: A child is not spoiled by praise and encouragement. Cecil G. Osborne says it well, "Perhaps once in a hundred years a person may be ruined by excessive praise. But surely once every minute someone dies inside for the lack of it."

The writer of Hebrews challenges all to "…see how inventive we can be in encouraging love and helping out" (10:25). The old saying that "Sticks and stones may break my bones but words will never hurt me" is simply untrue. Words can hurt. And words can heal.

Words of encouragement and celebration spur children on toward their highest potential. So Dads, how about a cheer for that child of yours? "Two bits, four bits, six bits a dollar, all for *your child* stand up and holler!"

The sweetest of all sounds is praise.

Xenophon

...as a father deals with his own children, encouraging, comforting and urging you to live lives worthy of God....
I Thessalonians 2:11-12

Celebrate your children's achievements.

Anonymous

Studies have shown that for every negative thing you say to a child, you must say four positive things just to keep the balance.

J. Allan Petersen

Children are not so different from kites. Children were created to fly. But they need wind, the undergirding and strength that comes from unconditional love, encouragement, and prayer.

Gigi Graham Tchividjian

For I am confident of this very thing, that He who began a good work in you will perfect it....
Philippians 1:6 NASB

Treat a man as he is and
he will remain as he is.
Treat a man as he can and
should be, and he will
become as he can and
should be.

Goethe

*...Eye hath not seen, nor ear heard,
neither have entered into the heart of man,
the things which God hath prepared
for them that love Him.
I Corinthians 2:9 KJV*

Our young people need to know
we have discovered the seeds of greatness
within them.

Unknown

Kids really respond to praise and
encouragement. I try to praise my kids
at least twenty-five times a day.

Josh McDowell

They say you can't live by bread alone,
but I can live on compliments.

Mark Twain

Praise your children openly,
reprove them secretly.

W. Cecil

*Let no unwholesome word proceed
from your mouth....
Ephesians 4:29 NLT*

Associate with those who help you believe
in yourself.

Brooks Robinson

Therefore encourage one another
and build each other up...

Paul the Apostle

Keep away from people who try to belittle
your ambitions. Small people always do that,
but the really great people make you feel
that you, too, can become great.

Mark Twain

*...[Barnabus] encouraged them all to remain
true to the Lord with all their hearts.
Acts 11:23*

Encouragement is more than hollow praise; it is urging others to hold fast to the principles of faith.

Unknown

...in Christ we who are many form one body and each member belongs to all the others....
Romans 12:5

When someone does something good,
applaud! You'll make two people happy.

Sam Goldwyn

If you are in the business of affirming
your teen, you may be pleasantly surprised
to hear your teen get into the business
of affirming you.

Gilbert Beers

We can either grace our children, or damn
them with unrequited wounds which
never seem to heal. Men, as Fathers,
you have such power!

R. Kent Hughes

A cheerful look brings joy to the heart,
and good news gives health....
Proverbs 15:30

8

School's In

A father's inescapable responsibility is the guidance and discipline he must provide for his child. The apostle Paul charges fathers to bring up children "in the nurture and admonition of the Lord."

A father's influence can hardly be overstated. As the old English proverb reminds us, "One father is more than a hundred school masters." Thus Dads have a wonderful opportunity to raise their children "in the way they should go."

So Dads, teach your children well. And remember that the kids you're raising belong to you *and* to God. God has big plans for all His children; it's your job to help.

Life doesn't come with an instruction book — that's why we have fathers.

H. Jackson Brown, Sr.

These commandments that I give you today are to be on your hearts. Impress them upon your children....
Deuteronomy 6:6-7

The primary values, attitudes, skills, and competencies that my children will grow up with will be learned — or not learned — in my home.

Tim Hansel

To be successful in the family, the father must have the welfare of each family member at heart, and his decisions and plans must be based upon what is best for them.

Helen Andelin

If we do not teach our children, society will. And they — and we — will live with the results.

Stephen Covey

*...He commanded our forefathers
to teach their children....
Psalm 78:5*

Let us look upon
our children, let us love
them and train them, as
children of the covenant
and children of the
promise. These are
the children of God.

Andrew Murray

*Train a child in the way he should go, and
when he is old he will not turn from it.*
Proverbs 22:6

Train your child in the way in which
you know you should have gone yourself.

C. H. Spurgeon

Training is not telling, not teaching,
not commanding, but something higher
than all of these. It is not only telling a child
what to do, but also showing him how to do it
and seeing that it is done.

Andrew Murray

The best way for a man to train up a child
in the way he should go is to travel
that way himself.

Unknown

*The father of a righteous man has great joy;
he who has a wise son delights in him.
Proverbs 23:24*

There are two lasting
bequests we can hope
to give our children.
One of these is roots;
the other, wings.

Hodding Carter

And all thy children shall be taught of the Lord;
and great shall be the peace of thy children.
Isaiah 54:13 KJV

Plant the seeds of spiritual truth so that
they grow in your child's fertile mind —
and bear good fruit.

Rita Schweitz

Of all the gifts that a parent can give a child,
the gift of learning to make good choices
is the most valuable and long-lasting.

Pat Holt and Grace Ketterman

Each child is unique, a special creation
of God with talents, abilities, personality,
preference, dislikes, potentials, strengths,
weaknesses, and skills that are his or her
own. As parents, we must seek to identify
these in each of our children and help them
become the persons God intended.

Dave Veerman

*All discipline for the moment seems not to be
joyful, but sorrowful; yet to those who have
been trained by it, afterwards it yields the
peaceful fruit of righteousness.*
Hebrews 12:11 NASB

The goal of disciplining
our children is to
encourage their growth
as respectful, responsible,
self-disciplined
individuals.

Don H. Highlander

Discipline your son and he will give you peace;
he will bring delight to your soul.
Proverbs 29:17

The child that never learns to obey
his parents in the home will not obey God
or man out of the home.

Susanna Wesly

An infallible way to make your child
miserable is to satisfy all his demands.

Henry Home (Lord Kames)

Discipline does not break a child's spirit
half as often as the lack of it
breaks a parent's heart.

Unknown

Life is tons of discipline.

Robert Frost

*For the commandment is a lamp; and the law
is light; and reproofs of instruction
are the way of life.
Proverbs 6:23 KJV*

Love and discipline are the foundation
of training your child.

J. Allen Peterson

There is a balance between firmness
and tenderness that good fathers constantly
try to achieve.

Steve Farrow

A man's children and his garden both
reflect the amount of weeding done
during the growing season.

Unknown

What children learn at home is what they
will take with them when they are grown.

Chuck Christensen

*He must manage his own family well and see
that his children obey him with proper respect.
I Timothy 3:4*

Our children are our most important guests:
They enter our home, ask for careful attention,
stay for awhile, and then leave to follow
their own way.

Henri Nouwen

A home is a place where we find direction.

Gigi Graham Tchividjian

A child educated only at school
is an undereducated child.

George Santayana

*Make them pure and holy by teaching them
your words of truth.
John 17:17 TLB*

The place for a child to learn religious faith is at home, in the bosom of a family where faith is lived and practiced.

Dick Van Dyke

Fathers, do not exasperate your children; instead, bring them up in the training and instruction of the Lord.
Ephesians 6:4

Whatever else maybe said about the home,
it is the bottom line of life, the anvil
upon which attitudes and convictions
are hammered out.

Chuck Swindoll

Character is not something highly valued
in this society, so it is most important that
the development of strong character be
emphasized and rewarded in the home.

Charles Stanley

The Christian home is the Master's workshop
where the processes of character-molding are
silently, lovingly, faithfully and successfully
carried on.

Richard Monckton Milnes

*You will be able to tell wonderful stories
to your children and grandchildren
about the marvelous things I am doing....
Exodus 10:2*

The best things you can give children, next to good habits, are good memories.

Sydney J. Harris

Hear, my son, your father's instruction....
Proverbs 1:8 NASB

9

Take For Example...

Every father is an example for his children. Dennis Rainey writes, "Every dad is the family role model whether he wants the job or not." Thankfully, God has given fathers a parenting guidebook that never fails — The Holy Bible.

The Bible exhorts fathers to become positive role models for their children: "...in everything set them an example by doing what is good" (Titus 2:7).

The choice is yours, Dad: You can be a good example for your kids or a not-so-good one. But make no mistake, you *will* be an example. So why not do yourself and your family an enormous favor: Be the kind of example that God wants for His children — and for yours.

You can't do much about your ancestors but you can influence your descendants enormously.

Anonymous

You became imitators of us and of the Lord….
I Thessalonians 1:7

Not only should we teach values, but we
should live them. My kids pay a lot more
attention to what I do than what I say.
A sermon is better lived than preached.

J. C. Watts

You cannot not model. It's impossible.
People will see your example — positive
or negative — as a pattern for the way
life is lived.

Stephen Covey

The power of example in a parent does more
to train a child than any other single thing.

Larry Christenson

*...leaving us an example, that ye should
follow his steps.
I Peter 2:21 KJV*

His heritage to his children wasn't words or possessions, but an unspoken treasure, the treasure of his example as a man and a father.

Will Rogers, Jr.

I learned from the example of my father that the manner in which one endures what must be endured is more important than the thing that must be endured.

Dean Acheson

I learned from my father how to work. I learned from him that work is life and life is work, and work is hard.

Philip Roth

Be ye doers of the word, and not hearers only. James 1:22 KJV

The world is blessed most by men who do things, and not by those who merely talk about them.

James Oliver

*For you yourselves know how you ought
to follow our example, because we did not act
in an undisciplined manner among you….
II Thessalonians 3:7 NASB*

Children have more need of models
than of critics.

Joseph Joubert

Remember, when your child has a tantrum,
don't have one of your own.

Dr. J. Kuriansky

An ounce of loving role modeling is worth
a pound of parental pressure.

Gilbert Beers

*…in order to offer ourselves as a model for
you, that you might follow our example.
II Thessalonians 3:9 NASB*

To become a father is easy; to be one is difficult.

American Proverb

*...and live a life of love, just as Christ loved us
and gave himself up for us....*
Ephesians 5:2

Like father, like son.

Unknown

The most important thing a father can do
for his children is love their mother.

Kirk Douglas and Theodore Hesburgh

For many little girls, life with father
is a dress rehearsal for love and marriage.

David Jeremiah

My father is the standard by which all
subsequent men in my life have been judged.

Kathryn McCarthy Graham

*Be their ideal; let them follow the way you
teach and live; be a pattern for them in your
love, your faith, and your clean thoughts.
I Timothy 4:12 TLB*

Our children observe us all day long, at our best and at our worst. Much of what they learn comes simply from living with us and observing us.

Shirley Suderman

…You were the model of perfection,
full of wisdom and perfect in beauty.
Ezra 28:12

Nothing is so potent as the silent influence
of a good example.

James Kent

Example is a lesson that all can read.

Gilbert West

Parents should make sure their lights
shine at home.

John Whitehead

*Be ye followers of me even
as I also am of Christ.
I Corinthians 11:1 KJV*

Children will not always listen to you, but they will always imitate you.

Edwin Louis Cole

...but be thou an example of the believers, in word, in conversation, in charity, in spirit, in faith, in purity.
I Timothy 4:12 KJV

The imprint of the parent remains forever
on the life of the child.

C. B. Eavey

Don't worry that your children never listen
to you; worry that they are
always watching you.

Robert Fulghum

Values are not taught to our children,
they are caught by them.

Unknown

*So be careful how you act; these are
difficult days.
Ephesians 5:15 TLB*

10

Walk the Talk

It has been said that the best way to teach character is to have it around the house. Fathers, take note: The people who live under your roof have a way of knowing whether or not you are who you say you are.

God promises to bless the man of integrity: "A righteous man who walks in his integrity — how blessed are his sons after him" (Proverbs 20:7 NASB).

Fathers, remember that it's not enough to "talk the talk"; you must also "walk the walk." The following pages show how.

When you were born, you cried and the world rejoiced! Live your live in such a manner that when you die, the world cries and you rejoice.

Old Indian Saying

God-loyal people, living honest lives, make it much easier for their children.
Proverbs 20:7 THE MESSAGE

A man ought to live so that everybody knows he is a Christian, and most of all, his family ought to know.

D. L. Moody

K ids aren't looking for perfect parents, but they are looking for honest and growing ones.

Howard Hendricks

T he measure of a man is not what he does on Sunday, but rather who he is Monday through Saturday.

Unknown

M aintaining your integrity in a world of sham is no small accomplishment.

Wayne Oates

*A truthful witness gives honest testimony,
but a false witness tells lies.
Proverbs 12:17*

Make your deeds follow your words.
Keep your actions in line with your values.
Keep your commitment to self and others,
and speak truth.

Stephen Covey

If you tell the truth, you don't have
to remember anything.

Mark Twain

Live your life in such a way that you would
not be ashamed to sell your parrot
to the town gossip.

Will Rogers

*Let us hold fast the profession of our faith
without wavering....
Hebrews 10:23 KJV*

In matters of style, swim with the current; in matters of principle, stand like a rock.

Thomas Jefferson

He holds victory in store for the upright….
Proverbs 2:7

Try not to become men of success. Rather,
become men of value.

Albert Einstein

Show class, have pride, and display character.
If you do, winning will take care of itself.

Bear Bryant

We are what we believe we are.

Benjamin Cardozo

*Man looks at the outward appearance, but the
Lord looks at the heart.
I Samuel 16:7*

Character is like the foundation of a house:
It lies beneath the surface and
everything else rests upon it.

Unknown

Character is much easier kept than recovered.

Thomas Paine

Character is what you are in the dark.

Dwight L. Moody

If I take care of my character, my reputation
will take care of itself.

D. L. Moody

The integrity of the upright shall guide them....
Proverbs 11:3

Sow an action and
you reap a habit;
Sow a habit and
you reap a character;
Sow a character and
you reap a destiny.

William James

In your teaching show integrity...
Titus 2:7

We can talk about faith, but what we live
shows the true faith behind the words.

Jay Kesler

Leadership must be demonstrated,
not announced.

Fran Tarkenton

We are effective only when we have integrity,
when our actions are in line with our values.

Stephen Covey

Personal honor is the mortar that holds
the bricks of life in place.

Stephen Covey

*Let us not become weary of doing good, for at
the proper time, we will reap a harvest if
we do not give up.*
Galatians 6:9

The process is as important as the product.

Stephen Covey

For when the one Great Scorer comes to write against your name, He marks not that you won or lost, but how you played the game.

Grantland Rice

In reality, the ends and the means, the destination and the journey are the same.

Stephen Covey

From good parents comes a good son.

Aristotle

A good tree cannot bear bad fruit....
Matthew 7:18

11

Gentleness and Respect

The Golden Rule is a golden rule: "Do unto others as you would have them do unto you" (Matthew 7:12). This is a rule for all ages — and for all fathers.

If children are to respect parents, parents must also respect children. Terence wrote, "It is better to bind your children to you by a feeling of respect, and by gentleness, than by fear."

The very best dads rule not by fear but by respect; here's how they do it...

Respect is not a one-way street;
    everyone is made in the image of God.

Josh McDowell

He that will have his son have respect
    for him and his orders, must himself have
    a great reverence for his son.

John Locke

We need to be careful that we in no way
    make light of our children's problems.

Josh McDowell

Something that has really helped me
    communicate with my kids is to ask
    their opinions.

Josh McDowell

*As a father has compassion on his children,
    so the Lord has compassion on those
    who fear him.
    Psalm 89:26*

Home is the place where the great are small and the small are great.

Robert Savage

God is opposed to the proud.
But gives grace to the humble.
James 4:6 NASB

Parents can show respect as their teens
begin to express independence by allowing
them to be the unique individuals
God made them to be.

Ted Engstrom

The way you see people is the way you treat
them. And the way you treat them is what
they become.

Goethe

If you want to get the best out of someone,
you must look for the best that is in him.

Unknown

When children know they are valued,
then they feel valuable.

M. Scott Peck

*Jesus said, "Let the little children come to me,
and do no hinder them, for the kingdom of
heaven belongs to such as these."*
Matthew 19:14

As we accept our children, we free them
to be who they are in a world that is trying
to tell them every day to be someone else.

Tim Hansel

You cannot teach a child to take care of
himself unless you will let him try. He will
make mistakes; and out of these mistakes
will come his wisdom.

Henry Ward Beecher

You don't raise heroes; you raise sons. And
if you treat them like sons, they'll turn out to
be heroes, even if it's just in your own eyes.

Walter Schirra, Sr.

*Each of you must take responsibility for doing
the creative best you can with your own life.
Galatians 6:5 THE MESSAGE*

We need to be patient with our children in the same way God is patient with us.

Renee Jordan

Be merciful, just as your Father is merciful.
Luke 6:36 NASB

It is better to bind your children to you
by a feeling of respect and by gentleness
than fear.

Terence

If a child lives with friendliness, he learns
that the world is a nice place in which to live.

Unknown

People don't care how much you know
until they know how much you care.

Unknown

Fathers, do not exasperate your children,
so that they will not lose heart.
Colossians 3:21 NASB

If a lion's roar isn't getting you any place, try a bear hug.

Anonymous

...Love is kind....
I Corinthians 13:4

Never mistake kindness for weakness.

Red Skelton

Nothing is so strong as gentleness,
nothing so gentle as real strength.

St. Francis de Sales

A gentleman is a gentle man.

Unknown

...thy gentleness hath made me great.
Psalm 18:35 KJV

If you want your child to accept your values when he reaches his teen years, then you must be worthy of his respect during his younger days.

James Dobson

...conduct yourselves in a manner worthy of the gospel of Christ....
Philippians 1:27

12

Got a Minute?

Family should be a priority for every dad. And, of course, anything that is a high priority demands our time. Stephen Covey, understanding the importance of "family time", warned, "To those who would say, 'We don't have time to do these things!', I would say, 'You don't have time not to!'"

Many hands grab for the time of dads, but the most precious hand is the hand of his child. Ephesians makes this point emphatically: "Don't be fools; be wise; make the most of every opportunity you have for doing good" (5:16 TLB).

Please don't be fooled, dads: *quality* time is *quantity* time. As you read the quotations and verses in this chapter, you will be motivated to make more time for your family. But while you're reading, if you hear one of your children say, "Hey, dad, have you got a minute?", feel free to put the book down. You've got more important things to do.

Seek God first, and the things you want will seek you.

Unknown

But seek ye first the kingdom of God, and his righteousness; and all these things shall be added unto you.
Matthew 6:33 KJV

No nation can be destroyed while it possesses
a good home life.

J. G. Holland

I would rather be a nobody in the world
but be somebody to my kids.

Patrick Morley

When you raise your children, you are also
raising your grandchildren. Patterns tend
to persist.

Stephen Covey

*...but as for me and my house,
we will serve the Lord.
Joshua 24:15*

It takes time to be a good father. It takes effort — trying, failing, and trying again.

Tim Hansel

Whatever you do, work at it with all your heart....
Colossians 3:23

Every calling is great when greatly pursued.
Unknown

Know what's most important
and give it all you've got.
Lee Iacocca

Things which matter most must never be
at the mercy of things which matter least.
Stephen Covey

*Acknowledge the God of your Father, and serve
him with wholehearted devotion....
I Corinthians 28:9*

I have decided not to let my time be used up by people to whom I make no difference while I neglect those for whom I am irreplaceable.

Tony Campolo

If anyone will not welcome you or listen to your words, shake the dust off your feet when you leave that home or town.
Matthew 10:14

He knew without a doubt that in wife
and child he had the only treasures
that really mattered anyway.

Lewis Grizzard

If I were starting my family life over again,
I would give first priority to my wife and
children, not to my work.

Richard Halverson

Wife and family come before business,
ministry, or career. God comes before
wife and family.

Edwin Louis Cole

*Do not store up for yourselves treasures
on earth. But store up for yourselves
treasures in heaven....
Matthew 6:19-20*

Whole-life stewardship means putting the purposes of God at the very center of our lives and families.

Tom Sine

Many are the plans of man's heart, but it is the Lord's purpose that prevails.
Proverbs 19:21

The only way to get this world back on track is to go back to the basics: How we raise our kids.

Lee Iacocca

If you bungle raising your children, I don't think whatever else you do well matters much.

Jacquelyn Kennedy

There is no failure that can alter the course of human events more than failing a family.

Eleanor McGovern

Train up a child in the way he should go,
Even when he is old he will not
depart from it.
Proverbs 22:6 NASB

Too much love never spoils children. Children become spoiled when we substitute "presents" for "presence."

Dr. Anthony P. Witham

...leaders, servants of the church, must be attentive to their children.
I Timothy 3:1,4,12 THE MESSAGE

To talk about parenting without involvement
is like talking about a business venture
without investment.

Gilbert Beers

When you have children, it is not enough
to put a roof over their heads, food in their
bellies, braces on their teeth, stereo head-
phones on their ears, $35 jeans on their
bodies, and combs in their back pockets.
You also have to DO things with them.

D. L. Stewart

*Teach them to your children, talking about
them when you sit at home and when you
walk along the road, when you lie down
and when you get up.*
Deuteronomy 11:19

Prime-time parents are parents who consider every minute with their children a prime time to communicate the message of parental love, interest, and care.

Kay Kuzma

*...make the most of every opportunity
you have for doing good....
Ephesians 5:16 TLB*

Children spell "love" — T-I-M-E.

Dr. Anthony P. Witham

I don't buy the cliché that quality time is the most important thing. If you don't have enough quantity, you won't get quality.

Leighton Ford

No test of a man's true character is more conclusive than how he spends his time and his money.

Patrick Morley

There's a right time for everything on earth:
a right time to love....
Ecclesiastes 2:1,8 THE MESSAGE

When we love something it is of value to us,
and when something is of value to us we
spend time with it, time enjoying it and time
taking care of it. Got a minute? So it is
when we love children; we spend time
admiring them and taking care of them.
We give them our time.

M. Scott Peck

To be in your children's memories tomorrow,
you have to be in their lives today.

Unknown

My dad and I hunted and fished together.
How could I get angry at this man
who took the time to be with me?

James Dobson

They are more precious than gold....
Psalm 19:10

The best gift parents can give children is themselves.

Annie Laurie Von Tun

*Give me your heart, my son, and let your eyes
delight in my ways.
Proverbs 23:26 NASB*

Index of Quoted Sources

About the Author

Jim Gallery lives and writes in Middle Tennessee. He serves as senior editor for both Brighton Books and Walnut Grove Press. In addition, Jim is a sought-after speaker and lecturer.

Jim is a graduate of the University of South Florida and the New Orleans Baptist Theological Seminary. He is the father of two children. He is the author of *God Can Handle It, God Can Handle It ...for Teenagers*, and *The Wisdom of the Irish*.

The *God Can Handle It* Series

God Can Handle It is a series published by Brighton Books. Each title features inspirational quotations and relevant scripture passages. The series includes:

God Can Handle It
>> by Jim Gallery

God Can Handle It... Day by Day
>> by S. M. Henriques

Gad Can Handle It ... for Kids
>> by S. M. Henriques

God Can Handle It...for Teenagers
>> by Julie & Jim Gallery

God Can Handle It ...for Mothers
>> by Carlene Ward

God Can Handle It ...for Fathers
>> by Jim Gallery

God Can Handle It ... Marriage
>> by S. M. Henriques

God Can Handle It ...for Graduates
>> by Criswell Freeman

For more information, call 1-800-256-8584.